Bond

Fourth papers

10–11+ years

Michellejoy Hughes

Comprehension

Nelson Thornes

Published in 2009 by:
Nelson Thornes Ltd
Delta Place
27 Bath Road
CHELTENHAM
GL53 7TH
United Kingdom

12 13 / 10 9 8 7 6

A catalogue record for this book is available from the British Library

ISBN 978 1 4085 0401 7

Illustrations by Angela Knowles
Page make-up by Pantek Arts Ltd, Maidstone, Kent

Printed and bound in Egypt by Sahara Printing Company

Acknowledgements

Extract from *Black Beauty* by Anna Sewell sourced from www.childrensnursery.org.
uk; Extract from 'Edward Lear's Nonsense Books complete set' (online version)
The Owl and the Pussy-Cat sourced from www.childrensnursery.org.uk; Extract
from 'Edward Lear's Nonsense Books complete set' (online version) *The Jumblies*
sourced from www.childrensnursery.org.uk; Extract from *Birds of the Air* by
Arabella Buckley sourced from www.mainlesson.com; Extract from *Grandfather's
Chair* by Nathaniel Hawthorne sourced from www.gutenberg.org; Extract from
Stories of the Ancient Greeks by Charles D. Shaw sourced from www.mainlesson.
com; Extract from *The Life of the Spider* by Jean Henri Fabre sourced from
 www.mainlesson.com; Extract from *Historical Tales: Russian* by Charles Morris
sourced from www.mainlesson.com; Extract from 'The Questing Beast' in *King
Arthur Tales of the Round Table* edited by Andrew Lang, sourced from
www.sacred-texts.com.

Every effort has been made to trace the copyright holders, but if any have been
inadvertently overlooked the publishers will be pleased to make the necessary
arrangement at the first opportunity.

Before you get started

About Bond

Bond is the leading name in practice for 11+ and other selective school exams (e.g. 7+, 12+, 13+, CEE), as well as for general practice in key learning skills. The series provides resources across the 5–13 years age range for English and maths and 6–12 years for verbal reasoning and non-verbal reasoning. Bond's English resources are also ideal preparation for teacher assessments at Key Stages 1 and 3, as well as for Key Stage 2 SATs.

About comprehension

Comprehension is a vital life skill. It involves the ability to critically read and understand written material and then to take or use relevant information from it. This skill is developed in children from an early age; consequently comprehension exercises form a core component of most English exams and assessments in school.

To test the breadth of a child's comprehension ability, exams may present one or more extracts taken from works of fiction (i.e. novels), poetry, playscripts or non-fiction (i.e. biographies, leaflets, advertisements, newspaper and magazine articles). Questions are likely to range from those that require direct, literal answers (e.g. *'What colour was the girl's coat?'*) to those that, with increasing levels of complexity, involve inferring information and offering a personal opinion (e.g. *'Why did Tom decide to put the money back?'; 'How do you think he felt when he realised that the money had gone?'*).

Children are likely to face a range of different comprehension tasks throughout Key Stages 1–3, particularly in English end-of-year assessments, Key Stage 2 SATs and 11+ (as well as other selective) English exams. Both wide reading and regular, focused comprehension practice are therefore essential for success.

What does the book contain?

- **10 papers** – providing comprehension practice at fiction, non-fiction and poetry. Each test includes one or more passages to read, followed by questions. The number of questions in a paper may vary but each test is worth a total of 35 marks. The comprehension texts and questions have been pitched at the level of a typical 11+ exam.

- **Tutorial links** throughout – – this icon appears in the margin next to the questions. It indicates links to the relevant sections in *The secrets of Comprehension*, our invaluable guide that explains all key aspects of comprehension.

- **Scoring devices** – there are score boxes in the margins and a Progress Chart on page 44.

- **Answers** – located in an easily-removed central pull-out section.

How can you use this book?

Flexibility is one of the great strengths of the Bond series. These comprehension books can therefore be used at home, in school and by tutors to:

- set timed exercises – for each paper allow around 10 minutes to read the extract(s), followed by 30 minutes to answer the questions; this will provide good practice for 11+ (and other exam) time frames
- provide regular, bite-sized practice
- highlight strengths and weaknesses
- identify individual needs
- set homework
- help build a complete 11+ English preparation strategy alongside other Bond resources (see below).

It is best to start at the beginning and work through the papers in order. If you are using the book as part of a careful run-in to the 11+, we suggest that you also have these other Bond resources close at hand:

The secrets of Comprehension: this practical handbook is an essential support for *Bond Comprehension 10–11+ years*. *The secrets of Comprehension* clearly explains to children how to read and understand a text, how to approach the core question types and how to assess their own answers. The margin icons in *Bond Comprehension 10–11+ years* indicate which questions are cross-referenced to the relevant sections of this handbook.

Bond Assessment Papers in English: these graded books provide lots of timed practice at comprehension, spelling, grammar and vocabulary work, in line with the scope of 11+ (and other) English exams.

How to do ... 11+ English: the subject guide that explains all aspects of 11+ English.

The Parents' Guide to the 11+: the step-by-step guide to the whole 11+ experience. It clearly explains the 11+ process, provides guidance on how to assess a child and helps you to set a complete action plan for a strategic run-in to the exam.

See the inside front cover for more details of these books.

What does a child's score mean and how can it be improved?

It is unfortunately impossible to guarantee that a child will pass the 11+ English exam (or any comprehension test) if they achieve a certain score on a practice paper. Success on the day will depend on a host of factors, including the performance of the other children. However, we can give some guidance on what a score indicates and how to improve it.

If children colour in the Progress Chart (page 44), this will give an indication of performance in percentage terms. The Next Steps Planner inside the back cover will then help you to decide what to do next. It is always valuable to go over incorrect answers with children. If they are having trouble with any particular question type, follow the tutorial links to *The secrets of Comprehension* for step-by-step explanations and further practice.

Don't forget the website…!

Visit www.bond11plus.co.uk for lots of free resources, advice and information about Bond, the 11+ and helping children to do their best.

Key words

adjective	a word that describes somebody or something
alliteration	a repetition of the same sound *five funny frogs*
conjunction	a word used to link sentences, phrases or words *and, but*
connective	a word or words that join clauses or sentences
grammar rule	a rule that we apply to a word when adding a prefix or suffix, e.g. reply – take off the y and add ies to make replies
homophone	a word that has the same sound as another but a different meaning or spelling *right / write*
narrator	a person who is telling a story
noun	a word for somebody or something
onomatopoeia	a word that echoes a sound associated with its meaning *hiss*
past tense	form of a verb showing that something has already happened
preposition	a word that relates other words to each other *the book on the table*
present tense	form of a verb showing something happening now
pronoun	a word used to replace a noun
simile	an expression to describe what something is like *as cold as ice*
suffix	a group of letters added to the end of a word *ly, ful*
superlative	describes the limit of a quality (adjective or adverb) *most / least* or *shortest*
synonym	a word with the same or very similar meaning to another word *quick – fast*
verb	a 'doing' or 'being' word

Paper 1

Chapter 1 My Early Home

The first place that I can well remember was a large, pleasant meadow with a pond of clear water in it. Some shady trees leaned over it, and rushes and water-lilies grew at the deep end. Over the hedge on one side we looked into a plowed field, and on the other we looked over a gate at our master's house, which stood by the roadside; at the top of the meadow was a grove of fir-trees, and at the bottom a 5 running brook, overhung by a steep bank.

While I was young I lived upon my mother's milk, as I could not eat grass. In the daytime I ran by her side, and at night I lay down close by her. When it was hot we used to stand by the pond in the shade of the trees, and when it was cold we had a warm shed near the grove. 10

As soon as I was old enough to eat grass, my mother used to go out to work in the daytime, and come back in the evening.

There were six young colts in the meadow besides me; they were older than I was; some were nearly as large as grown-up horses. I used to run with them, and had great fun: we used to gallop all together round and round the field, as hard as 15 we could go. Sometimes we had rather rough play, for they would frequently bite and kick, as well as gallop.

One day, when there was a good deal of kicking, my mother whinnied to me to come to her, and then she said:

"I wish you to pay attention to what I am going to say to you. The colts who live 20 here are very good colts, but they are cart-horse colts, and, of course, they have not learned manners. You have been well-bred and well-born; your father has a great name in these parts, and your grandfather won the cup two years at the Newmarket races; your grandmother had the sweetest temper of any horse I ever knew, and I think you have never seen me kick or bite. I hope you will grow up gentle and 25 good, and never learn bad ways; do your work with a good will, lift your feet up well when you trot, and never bite or kick even in play."

I have never forgotten my mother's advice; I knew she was a wise old horse, and our master thought a great deal of her. Her name was Duchess, but he called her Pet.

Our master was a good, kind man. He gave us good food, good lodging and 30 kind words; he spoke as kindly to us as he did to his little children. We were all fond of him and my mother loved him very much. When she saw him at the gate she would neigh with joy, and trot up to him.

From *Black Beauty* by Anna Sewell

1 The **narrator** is a young boy. Do you agree with this statement? Support your answer with evidence from the text.

B 2

_____

2

_____

2 What do you think is meant by the term 'rough play', as used in the extract?

B 2

_____

1

_____

3 Give an alternative for each word as it is used in the context of the text.

B 2

a whinnied (line 18) _____   **b** grove (line 5) _____

4

c temper (line 24) _____   **d** lodging (line 30) _____

4 Find THREE pieces of text that refer to the age of the **narrator**.

B 2

_____

_____

3

_____

5 Give THREE ways in which the **narrator** is different from his friends.

B 2

_____

_____

_____

3

_____

6 Find FOUR pieces of text that show why Duchess might love the master.

B 2

_____

_____

_____

_____

4

7 What does the **narrator's** mother mean when she refers to 'bad ways'?

B 2

_____

1

_____

8 Describe FIVE traits that the **narrator's** mother wishes him to have.

a _____

b _____

c _____

d _____

e _____ **5**

9 Why do you think the **narrator's** mother tells him about his family lineage?

_____

_____

_____ **2**

10 Tick the THREE statements that are true.

A His father won two cups at Newmarket. ☐

B Water-lilies can grow in deep water. ☐

C His grandmother's name was Duchess. ☐

D There were at least eight of them in the field. ☐

E The warm shed was near the top of the meadow. ☐

F The running brook was at the top of the meadow. ☐ **3**

11 Find an example of each of the following parts of speech in this sentence.

'The first place that I can well remember was a large, pleasant meadow with a pond of clear water in it.'

a **pronoun** _____   b **verb** _____

c **adjective** _____   d **preposition** _____ **4**

12 Write these words in their **present tense** form.

a had _____   b thought _____

c spoke _____ **3**

The Owl and the Pussy-Cat

I.

The Owl and the Pussy-Cat went to sea
In a beautiful pea-green boat, They took
    some honey, and plenty of money,
Wrapped up in a five-pound note. The Owl
    looked up to the stars above,
And sang to a small guitar, "O lovely Pussy!
    O Pussy, my love,   5
What a beautiful Pussy you are, You are,
    You are! What a beautiful Pussy you are!"

II.

Pussy said to the Owl, "You elegant fowl!   10
How charmingly sweet you sing! Oh! let us be
    married! too long we have tarried:
But what shall we do for a ring?" They sailed away,
    for a year and a day,
To the land where the Bong-tree grows, And there in   15
    a wood a Piggy-wig stood
With a ring at the end of his nose, His nose, His
    nose, With a ring at the end of his nose.

III.

"Dear Pig, are you willing to sell for one shilling
Your ring?" Said the Piggy, "I will." So they took it   20
    away, and were married next day
By the Turkey who lives on the hill.
They dined on mince and slices of quince,
Which they ate with a runcible spoon; And hand in
    hand, on the edge of the sand,   25
They danced by the light of the moon, The moon,
    The moon, They danced by the light of the moon.

The Owl and the Pussy-Cat by Edward Lear

The Jumblies

I.

They went to sea in a Sieve, they did,
In a Sieve they went to sea: In spite of all
   their friends could say,
On a winter's morn, on a stormy day,
In a Sieve they went to sea! And when the   5
   Sieve turned round and round,
And every one cried, "You'll all be
   drowned!"
They called aloud, "Our Sieve ain't big,
But we don't care a button! we don't care a   10
   fig!
In a Sieve we'll go to sea!" Far and few,
   far and few, Are the lands where the
   Jumblies live; Their heads are green, and
   their hands are blue, And they went to   15
   sea in a Sieve.

II.

They sailed away in a Sieve, they did,
In a Sieve they sailed so fast, With only a
   beautiful pea-green veil
Tied with a ribbon, by way of a sail,   20
To a small tobacco-pipe mast; And every
   one said, who saw them go,
"O won't they be soon upset, you know!
For the sky is dark, and the voyage is long,
And, happen what may, it's extremely wrong 25
In a Sieve to sail so fast!" Far and few,
   far and few, Are the lands where the
   Jumblies live; Their heads are green, and
   their hands are blue, And they went to
   sea in a Sieve.   30

III.

The water it soon came in, it did,
The water it soon came in; So to keep them
   dry, they wrapped their feet
In a pinky paper all folded neat,
And they fastened it down with a pin. And   35
   they passed the night in a crockery-jar,
And each of them said, "How wise we are!
Though the sky be dark, and the voyage be
   long,
Yet we never can think we were rash or   40
   wrong,
While round in our Sieve we spin!" Far and
   few, far and few, Are the lands where the
   Jumblies live; Their heads are green, and
   their hands are blue, And they went to   45
   sea in a Sieve.

IV.

And all night long they sailed away;
And when the sun went down, They
   whistled and warbled a moony song
To the echoing sound of a coppery gong,   50
In the shade of the mountains brown. "O
   Timballo! How happy we are,
When we live in a Sieve and a crockery-jar!
And all night long, in the moonlight pale,
We sail away with a pea-green sail,   55
In the shade of the mountains brown!" Far
   and few, far and few, Are the lands where
   the Jumblies live; Their heads are green,
   and their hands are blue; And they went
   to sea in a Sieve.   60

V.

They sailed to the Western Sea, they did,
To a land all covered with trees, And they
   bought an owl, and a useful Cart,
And a pound of Rice, and a cranberry Tart,
And a hive of silvery Bees. And they bought 65
   a Pig, and some green Jack-daws,
And a lovely Monkey with lollipop paws,
And forty bottles of Ring-Bo-Ree,
And no end of Stilton Cheese. Far and few,
   far and few, Are the lands where the   70
   Jumblies live; Their heads are green, and
   their hands are blue; And they went to
   sea in a Sieve.

The Jumblies by Edward Lear

These questions are about *The Owl and the Pussy-Cat*.

1 Name THREE items that the owl and the pussy-cat took with them on their travels. `B 2`

_____

_____ `3`

2 What time of day was it when the owl and the pussy-cat first set sail? `B 2`

_____ `1`

3 Which animal suggested that there should be a wedding? `B 2`

_____ `1`

4 How many days were the animals at sea? `B 2`

_____ `1`

5 What do you think is meant by these words as they are used in the text? `B 2`

a tarried (line 12) _____

b quince (line 23) _____

c fowl (line 10) _____ `3`

6 Describe in your own words how they find a wedding ring. `B 3`

_____

_____

_____ `2`

7 Find FOUR **homophones** in this sentence. Write them, with their **homophone** partners, below. `B 2`

"Dear Pig, are you willing to sell for one shilling your ring?"

a _____ / _____   **b** _____ / _____

c _____ / _____   **d** _____ / _____ `4`

These questions are about *The Jumblies*.

8 Name TEN items that the Jumblies bought in the 'land all covered with trees'.

_____ _____ _____

_____ _____ _____

_____ _____ _____

_____

9 What time of the year was it when the Jumblies set sail?

_____

10 Name TWO things that they did to keep themselves dry.

_____

_____

11 What was attached to the mast?

_____

12 What did the Jumblies do at sunset?

_____

_____

_____

_____

13 What do you think is meant by these words as they are used in the text?

a voyage (verse II, line 24) _____

b warbled (verse IV, line 49) _____

c rash (verse III, line 40) _____

These questions are about both poems.

14 *The Owl and the Pussy-Cat* and *The Jumblies* are both 'nonsense' poems. Find SIX pieces of evidence to support this statement. You can take your evidence from either or both poems.

B 2

_____

_____

_____

_____

_____

_____

3

_____

15 Both poems are about a sea journey. Find another FOUR things that both poems have in common.

B 2

_____

_____

_____

2

_____

Now go to the Progress Chart to record your score!   Total   35

Bird-food in Winter

When Christmas is past and the real winter cold begins, the poor little birds often
have a hard time. So long as the weather is mild, the thrush picks out the slugs
and snails from their hiding-places in the walls and palings. The robin and the wren
bustle about, looking for seeds and insects. The little wagtails run about the lawns
wagging their tails, as they try to find a stray grub, or beetle. In the wood the tree-   5
creeper hunts for spiders and the eggs of insects in the bark of the trees, and the
nuthatches and pigeons feed under the beeches.

But after a while, when a hard frost comes, and snow lies deep on the ground,
the birds look very sad. The larks and the linnets crouch down under the banks of
the cornfields to keep warm. The thrushes fly from tree to tree to look for a   10
few mistletoe berries, now that all the others are eaten.
The chaffinches and the yellow-hammers fly round the
farmer's ricks, to pull out some grains of wheat or
oats, or grass seeds. The field-fares wander
sadly about in flocks.   15
The rooks, starlings, and
jackdaws fly from field to field
screaming and cawing as
they try to find some place where
the wind has blown the snow away
and they can peck in the furrows. The   20
lapwings, which you may know by the
feathers which stand up on the back of
their head, cry "peewit, peewit" mournfully,
as they journey to the sea-coast, where they   25
find food on the sands and mudflats at low tide.

It is sad to think how often little birds are starved to death. They do not so much
mind the cold, for you remember that the air under their feathers keeps them warm.
But in a hard winter they often die from want of food. If you pick up a dead robin,
starling, or rook after a long frost, you will find that the bones are only covered with   30
skin and feathers. Its flesh has all wasted away.

Now is your time to be kind to the birds which have sung to you all the summer.
They did good work then, eating the caterpillars and grubs, the wire-worms and
maggots, the slugs and snails, and keeping down the weeds by eating the seeds.
Now you can feed them, for a little while, till the frost and snow are gone.   35

You will learn to know a great many birds in this way, and you need only give
them a few scraps, which you can well spare. Some birds, you will remember, like
seeds and crumbs and green food. Others, which eat insects in the summer, will be
glad of a little gristle or fat.

So you must save up every scrap from breakfast, dinner, and supper, and keep it   40
for the next morning – crusts of bread, the crumbs off the table, cold potatoes, and
potato skins. You can get your mother to boil the potatoes in their skins, and then

the birds will like the peel. Perhaps, too, you may save some pieces of cabbage, some apple parings, and a little fat.

All this will make a nice dish for starving birds, if you chop it up and pour a little hot water over the crusts. And if you live on a farm you may be able to sweep up a few grains of corn in the stables, before they are thrown away with the manure. 45

Then clear the snow away in front of your door, throw the food down and go back out of sight. The birds will soon come, and in a few days they will even be waiting about for their morning meal before you bring it. 50

You must not forget to hang a piece of fat from the branch of a tree, so that you may see the tits hang head downwards on the string to peck at it. And if you hang up a bone with a little meat on it the starlings and jackdaws will come too.

Then remember that birds want to drink. You can put water for them in a pan, if you change it when it freezes. But if you can spare a few pence to buy a cocoa-nut, 55 you may make it serve two purposes.

Saw it across the middle, and scoop out all the white from one half. Bore two holes near the rim of this cup, and make a handle with a piece of string. Then hang it on a tree and put some water in it. The birds will sit on the rim and drink. And as they make it swing to and fro the water will not freeze. Then hang up the other half 60 in the same way, but leave the white inside. The little tomtits will peck away, and fight for the sweet food till it is all gone.

A number of birds will come – robins, chaffinches, sparrows, wrens, starlings, rooks, jackdaws, thrushes, and many others. You will be able to notice the difference between the big missel-thrush, with his white spotted breast, and the 65 smaller brown song-thrush. And if you put some nuts on the window-sill the nuthatch may come to fetch them if he lives near.

So you will see the birds more closely than you can at any other time, and next summer, when they sing in the trees, they will be old friends.

From Birds of the Air by Arabella Buckley

1 Use the information given in the first two paragraphs to help you complete this table.

B 2

Birds	Food they eat
Robin	
Wagtail	
Thrush	
Chaffinch	
Tree-creeper	

5

2 Explain how larks keep warm when there is snow on the ground.

B 2

_____

_____

1

3 Why is it that birds do not mind the cold?

B 2

_____

_____

1

4 Give TWO key factors that cause birds to die in winter.

B 2

_____

_____

2

5 How can birds be helpful to gardeners? Support your answer with at least THREE pieces of evidence from the text.

B 2

_____

_____

_____

_____

3

6 Explain, in your own words, TWO ways in which a cocoa-nut can be useful in the garden.

B 3

_____

_____

_____

2

7 Tick the TWO statements that are true.

B 2

A Birds like to eat potato skins. ☐

B Field-fares walk around in pairs. ☐

C A song-thrush has a white spotted breast. ☐

D Pigeons like to eat food beneath trees. ☐

E Starlings can easily find food beneath snow. ☐

2

8 Why do you think the author describes the lapwings' call as 'mournful' (line 24?)

B 2

_____

_____

2

9 Explain, in your own words, how the lapwings find food at the coast.

B 3

_____

_____

2

10 Which phrase, as used in the context of the extract, means the same as 'rush around'?

B 2

_____

_____

1

11 In the extract, the word 'hide' is written as 'hiding'. (line 3)

B 2

a Which grammar rule must be applied to 'hide' before adding the 'ing' **suffix**?

_____

_____

b Find another word in the text that has followed this rule. _____

2

12 Explain, in your own words, why water is more likely to freeze in a pan than in half a cocoa-nut.

B 3

_____

_____

2

13 What do you think is meant by these words as they are used in the text?

B 2

a bore (line 57) _____

b rim (line 58) _____

2

14 What type of reader do you think this text has been written for? Support your answer with evidence from the text.

B 2

_____

_____

2

13

15 Tick the TWO types of food that the author does not recommend as ingredients for birds' meals.

A Pieces of bread. ☐

B A range of insects. ☐

C Scraps of winter greens. ☐

D Apple peel. ☐

E Corn-on-the-cob. ☐

2

16 Birds only need feeding in the winter. How far do you agree with this statement? Refer to the text in your answer.

_____

_____

_____

_____

_____

_____

4

Now go to the Progress Chart to record your score! Total 35

14

Paper 4

Extract A

The Fox and the Crow

One day the sly, old fox went out for a walk when he saw a crow in the top of the
tree. The crow was the scruffiest old bird with tatty feathers and a scrawny head,
but she had an enormous chunk of cheese in her beak and the cheese smelled
so good to the hungry fox. The fox thought carefully about how he could get the
cheese and said to the crow: 5
   "Kind crow, clever crow, you are the most beautifully elegant bird in all of the
world. Your feathers are as glossy as ebony, your intelligence is greater than all
other creatures, but it is your voice, your unforgettable, beautiful voice that is
sweeter than the nightingale and as pretty as a picture. I do so love to hear your
voice so will you sing me your prettiest song?"   10
   The crow was delighted to hear such praise. She shook her tatty feathers, lifted
her scrawny head and opened her beak wide to begin her squawking. Down fell
the chunk of cheese into the open mouth of the crafty fox. He snapped his teeth
together. Snap! Snap! Snap! And the cheese was gone. The fox licked his lips and
looked up at the dismayed crow.   15
   "You silly crow. I am the cleverest creature in the whole world, for I knew how to
trick you. Your pride was your downfall and my prize fell down to me!"

Extract B

The Fox and the Cat

Now this same fox was boasting to a cat about how many ways he had for
escaping the enemy. He remarked, "Oh you're the stupidest cat. You can only climb
up trees, but I have a whole bag of tricks that makes me the brightest creature in
the whole world."
   At that, a pack of hunting dogs came bounding towards them with their teeth   5
gnashing hungrily and their eyes burning brightly. The clever cat scampered up the
tree and avoided the terrible onslaught. She looked down at the fox and said, "Well
this is my plan. What are you going to do?"
   The fox thought through all of his clever ways as the dogs got closer and closer
but alas, he was caught up in his own confusion and the dogs had their prey.   10

Extract C

The Fox and the Stork

The fox found that he got on well with a stork, so one day he invited the stork to
his home for a meal. The stork was very excited and turned up feeling very hungry.
The fox decided to play a cruel joke on the poor stork by serving some soup on a
shallow plate. The fox sat at the table licking up the soup saying, "Oh how delicious
this soup is, are you enjoying it, Stork?"   5

The stork had such a long beak that she couldn't eat any of the soup at all; she
could only dip the very end of her beak into it. The fox made the joke worse by
saying, "Oh Stork, I am sorry that you do not like my lovely soup. You have left all of
it! Perhaps you are not hungry?"

The stork calmly replied, "Please do not apologise, Fox, I am sure that your soup   10
is very tasty. I look forward to you coming to my house tomorrow as I am making a
fine stew."

The greedy fox looked forward to visiting the stork as he had heard about the
lovely food that she cooked. As he knocked on the stork's door he could smell the
most wonderful aroma and he licked his lips with glee. The stork let the fox in and   15
ushered him to the table. The fox could hardly wait as the clever stork brought to
the table two of the longest jars that the fox had ever seen, and they were full of the
tastiest stew. The stork could easily fit her long beak into the jar as she supped the
hot food. The fox could see and smell the food, but his snout would not fit into the
jar. All he could do was watch the stork consume the delightful fare.   20

"Ah my dear Fox," said the stork, "what goes around comes around!"

From *Aesop's fables*; adaptations by Michellejoy Hughes

These questions are about Extract A.

1 Why did the fox want the crow's cheese?

_____

2 Underline the TWO words from the list below that best describe the crow's
character.

humble   vain   modest   conceited   extravagant

3 Find an alternative word for these terms, as they are used in the text.

a dismayed (line 15) _____   b scrawny (line 12) _____

4 Each quote below is an example of a literary technique. Join each phrase to the
technique it represents.

a "as pretty as a picture ..."   **alliteration**

b "Snap! Snap! Snap! And the cheese was gone ..."   **simile**

c "Kind crow, clever crow ..."   **onomatopoeia**

16

5 Find another example of a **simile** in the text.

_____

B 2
1

These questions are about Extract B.

6 Underline the word in brackets that is closest in meaning to each word as it is used in the text.

B 2

a scampered (line 6)   (darted, sidled, crept, struggled, strode)

b alas (line 10)   (despite, sadly, because, regretful, although)

2

7 Find TWO **homophones** in this phrase. Write them, with their **homophone** partners, below.

B 2

'... he was caught up in his own confusion ...'

a _____ / _____   **b** _____ / _____

2

8 Explain the phrase 'a whole bag of tricks' (line 3, as used in the extract).

B 2

_____

_____

1

9 What do you think this tale teaches the reader?

B 3

_____

_____

_____

2

These questions are about Extract C.

B 2

10 Reread the phrase 'what goes around comes around' (line 21).

a Which literary technique is this phrase an example of? _____

1

b Explain what the phrase means in your own words.

_____

_____

2

11 Why do you think the stork is referred to as 'clever'? (line 16)

B 2

_____

_____

_____

2

These questions are about all three extracts.

12 These three tales are called 'fables'. Write your own definition of a fable.

B 2

_____

_____

13 Why do you think the author has used a fox in all three tales?

_____

_____

_____

_____

14 Use the information given in each tale to write a description of the fox in your own words. Refer to the text in your answer.

_____

_____

_____

_____

15 The fox thinks that the crow is vain, the cat is stupid and the stork has no feelings. Do you think his opinion of each animal is correct? Explain your answer.

_____

_____

_____

_____

_____

_____

16 The author includes several **superlatives** in the texts. Find THREE examples, one from each extract.

a From Extract A: _____

b From Extract B: _____

c From Extract C: _____

Chapter 1 Grandfather and the Children and the Chair

Grandfather had been sitting in his old arm-chair all that pleasant afternoon, while the children were pursuing their various sports far off or near at hand. Sometimes you would have said, "Grandfather is asleep;" but still, even when his eyes were closed, his thoughts were with the young people, playing among the flowers and shrubbery of the garden. 5

He heard the voice of Laurence, who had taken possession of a heap of decayed branches which the gardener had lopped from the fruit-trees, and was building a little hut for his cousin Clara and himself. He heard Clara's gladsome voice, too, as she weeded and watered the flower-bed which had been given her for her own. He could have counted every footstep that Charley took, as he trundled his wheelbarrow 10 along the gravel-walk. And though Grandfather was old and gray-haired, yet his heart leaped with joy whenever little Alice came fluttering, like a butterfly, into the room. Sire had made each of the children her playmate in turn, and now made Grandfather her playmate too, and thought him the merriest of them all.

At last the children grew weary of their sports, because a summer afternoon is 15 like a long lifetime to the young. So they came into the room together, and clustered round Grandfather's great chair. Little Alice, who was hardly five years old, took the privilege of the youngest, and climbed his knee. It was a pleasant thing to behold that fair and golden-haired child in the lap of the old man, and to think that, different as they were, the hearts of both could be gladdened with the same joys. 20

"Grandfather," said little Alice, laying her head back upon his arm, "I am very tired now. You must tell me a story to make me go to sleep."

"That is not what story-tellers like," answered Grandfather, smiling. "They are better satisfied when they can keep their auditors awake."

"But here are Laurence, and Charley, and I," cried cousin Clara, who was twice 25 as old as little Alice. "We will all three keep wide awake. And pray, Grandfather, tell us a story about this strange-looking old chair."

Now, the chair in which Grandfather sat was made of oak, which had grown dark with age, but had been rubbed and polished till it shone as bright as mahogany. It was very large and heavy, and had a back that rose high above Grandfather's white 30 head. This back was curiously carved in open work, so as to represent flowers, and foliage, and other devices, which the children had often gazed at, but could never understand what they meant. On the very tip-top of the chair, over the head of Grandfather himself, was a likeness of a lion's head, which had such a savage grin that you would almost expect to hear it growl and snarl. 35

The children had seen Grandfather sitting in this chair ever since they could remember anything. Perhaps the younger of them supposed that he and the chair had come into the world together, and that both had always been as old as they were now. At this time, however, it happened to be the fashion for ladies to adorn their drawing-rooms with the oldest and oddest chairs that could be found. 40 It seemed to cousin Clara that, if these ladies could have seen Grandfather's old chair, they would have thought it worth all the rest together. She wondered if it were not even older than Grandfather himself, and longed to know all about its history.

"Do, Grandfather, talk to us about this chair," she repeated.

"Well, child," said Grandfather, patting Clara's cheek, "I can tell you a great many stories of my chair. Perhaps your cousin Laurence would like to hear them too. They would teach him something about the history and distinguished people of his country which he has never read in any of his schoolbooks." 45

Cousin Laurence was a boy of twelve, a bright scholar, in whom an early thoughtfulness and sensibility began to show themselves. His young fancy kindled at the idea of knowing all the adventures of this venerable chair. He looked eagerly in Grandfather's face; and even Charley, a bold, brisk, restless little fellow of nine, sat himself down on the carpet, and resolved to be quiet for at least ten minutes, should the story last so long. 50

Meantime, little Alice was already asleep; so Grandfather, being much pleased with such an attentive audience, began to talk about matters that happened long ago. 55

From *Grandfather's Chair* by Nathaniel Hawthorne

1 List the children's names in age order, from oldest to youngest.

B 2

1

_____

2 Was Clara happy as she tended to the flower-bed? Explain your answer with reference to the text.

B 2

_____

_____

2

3 Tick the TWO statements that are true.

B 2

A The chair was worth a lot of money. ☐

B Grandfather had brown hair. ☐

C Clara and Laurence were cousins. ☐

D Alice slept during Grandfather's story. ☐

E Grandfather rarely sat in the chair. ☐

2

4 Explain, in your own words, why the children 'grew weary of their sports' (line 15).

B 3

_____

_____

_____

2

Answers will vary for questions that require children to answer in their own words. Possible answers to most of these questions are given in *italics*.

Paper 1

1 The statement is false; the narrator is a horse not a young boy. [1]
  [1] mark for including a piece of appropriate evidence such as, the narrator:
  • states that he eats grass (line 11)
  • refers to himself as a colt (line 13)
  • refers to his friends as grown-up horses (line 14)
  • states that he galloped around the field (line 15)
  • recalls that his mother referred to his grandmother as having the sweetest temper of any horse she ever knew (line 24)
  • recalls his mother's instruction to lift his feet when trotting (lines 26–27)
  • refers to his mother as a wise old horse (line 28)
  • states that his mother neighed and trotted over to their master (line 33)
2 Child's answer should refer to 'biting' or 'kicking'.
3 a *called*
  b *woodland*
  c *nature*
  d *accommodation*
4 [1] mark each for any three of these points:
  • 'The first place that I can well remember' (line 1) suggests a past, therefore he isn't a baby.
  • 'While I was young' (line 7) suggests that he is no longer young.
  • 'As soon as I was old enough to eat grass' (line 11) shows that he is no longer a baby.
  • 'There were six young colts in the meadow besides me' (line 13) shows his age in terms of horse development.
  • 'They were older than I was' (lines 13–14) shows his youth at that time in comparison with the other horses.
  • 'I have never forgotten my mother's advice' (line 28) shows he is now older than he was in the memory.
5 [1] mark for each point:
  • 'They were older than I was' (lines 13–14) shows the difference in age.
  • 'You have been well-bred' (line 22) shows the contrast between him and the cart-horse colts.

• 'well born; your father had a great name in these parts and your grandfather won the cup two years at the Newmarket races' (lines 22–24) shows his difference in pedigree.
6 [1] mark each for any four of these points:
  • 'Our master was a good, kind man' (line 30)
  • 'He gave us good food' (line 30)
  • He gave us 'good lodging' (line 30)
  • He gave us 'kind words' (line 31)
  • 'He spoke as kindly to us as he did to his little children' (line 31)
7 Child's answer may refer to one or more relevant terms such as: 'kicking', 'biting', 'roughness', 'not doing good work', 'not lifting his feet up well when trotting'.
8 [1] mark each for any five of these points:
  • To grow up gentle (line 25)
  • To grow up good (line 26)
  • Never to learn bad ways (line 26)
  • To do his work willingly (line 26)
  • To lift his feet up when trotting (lines 26–27)
  • Never to bite (line 27)
  • Never to kick (line 27)
9 [1] mark each for any two of these (or similar) points:
  • To remind him of his family (father, grandfather, grandmother, mother) (lines 22–25)
  • To inform him that he is well-bred/has breeding (line 22)
  • To encourage him to behave properly, as other generations had done (lines 24–25)
  • To explain the difference between himself and the cart-horse colts (lines 20–22)
  • To teach him the importance of manners (line 22)
10 B (lines 2–3), D (line 13), E (line 10)
11 a I / it
   b remember
   c first / large / pleasant / clear
   d in / with
12 a have
   b think
   c speak

Paper 2

1 [1] mark each for any three of these items: honey, plenty of money, five-pound note, guitar
2 night (line 5 refers to the stars)
3 Pussy (line 12)
4 366 days (or 367 if it's a leap year) (line 14)
5 a *delayed*, *waited*
  b *fruit*
  c *bird*

6 *The Owl and Pussy-cat find a pig that has a ring in its nose* [1] *and they buy the ring off him for one shilling* [1].

7 **a–d** [1] mark each for any four of these homophone sets:
dear / deer; you / yew or ewe; to / two or too; sell / cell; for / four; your / yore; ring / wring

8 [1/2] mark for each item listed in verse V:
an Owl, a Cart, a pound of Rice, a Cranberry Tart, a hive of Bees, a Pig, green Jackdaws, a Monkey, 40 bottles of Ring-Bo-Ree, Stilton Cheese

9 winter (verse I, line 4)

10 [1] mark for each point (verse III):
• They wrapped their feet in a pinky paper (lines 33–34)
• They spent the night in a crockery-jar (line 36)

11 a pea-green veil (verse II, line 19)

12 [1] mark for each point (verse IV):
• They whistled (line 49)
• They sang (line 49)
• They played a coppery gong (line 50)

13 **a** *journey*
b *sang*
c *reckless*

14 [1/2] mark each for any six of these points:
The Owl and the Pussy-Cat refers to:
• talking animals
• animals who go off sailing
• a guitar-playing owl
• an animal marriage
The Jumblies:
• go out to sea in a sieve
• have green heads and blue hands
• use a tobacco pipe as a mast
• spend the night in a crockery-jar
• buy strange items such as a monkey with lollipop paws
Both poems:
• include invented words (e.g. Bong-tree; Ring-Bo-Ree)

15 [1/2] mark each for any four of these (or similar) points:
Both poems refer to:
• a distant land
• musical instruments being played
• characters who sing
• an item that is a pea-green colour
• an owl
• a pig
• the moon
• items being purchased

Paper 3

1 [1] mark for each correctly completed list of food:
Robin – seeds, insects
Wagtail – grubs, beetles
Thrush – slugs, snails, mistletoe berries
Chaffinch – wheat, oats, grass seeds
Tree-creeper – spiders, eggs of insects

2 Child's answer should refer to larks crouching down under the banks of the cornfields.

3 Child's answer should refer to birds being kept warm by the air under their feathers.

4 [1] mark for each point:
• A lack of food (line 29)
• Their inability to reach food due to heavy frost and / or snow (lines 20–21)

5 [1] mark for each point:
• They sing to them in the summer.
• They eat insects / pests such as caterpillars, wire-worms, slugs and snails.
• They help to keep weeds down by eating the seeds.

6 *A cocoa-nut can be useful for holding water for birds to drink* [1] (line 59) *and it is also a good source of food for birds* [1] (lines 61–62).

7 A (line 43), D (line 7)

8 *The lapwings' call is described as mournful because there is very little food around for them to eat* [1] (line 24), *causing them to travel all the way to the coast to find food* [1] (lines 25–26).

9 *The lapwings look for food on the sands and mudflats at the coast* [1] (lines 25–26), *but they can only do this when the tide goes out and these areas become visible* [1] (line 26).

10 bustle (line 4)

11 **a** *When adding the 'ing' suffix to a root word that ends in an 'e', drop the 'e' then add the suffix.*
b starving (line 45) or paring (line 44)

12 *Water is more likely to freeze in a pan because it is a stationary object* [1]. *A cocoa-nut would swing about when birds perched on it, so the water inside it would move around and would therefore not freeze so easily* [1].

13 **a** *drill*
b *edge*

14 *This text has been written for children* [1] *because the author tells the reader to ask their mother to boil some potatoes* [1] (line 42).

15 B, E

16 [1] mark each for any four of these (or similar) points:

The text implies that winter is the worst season for birds in terms of finding food as it states that:

- in winter the 'poor little birds often have a hard time' (lines 1–2)
- before the hard frosts come, birds can find seeds and insects (lines 2–4)
- birds look 'sad' at this time of year (line 9)
- birds often starve to death in winter through lack of food (line 29)
- birds' flesh often wastes away (line 31)
- winter is the time for us all to be kind to the birds (line 32)
- many different types of bugs, grubs and seeds are readily available for birds in summer, suggesting that they do not need to be given additional food scraps at this time (lines 33–34)
- birds find it hard to locate food underneath frost and snow (line 35)

Paper 4

1 The cheese smelled so good [$^1/_2$] and the fox was hungry [$^1/_2$] (lines 3–4).

2 vain, conceited

3 a *shocked*
b *skinny*

4 A = a simile
B = onomatopoeia
C = alliteration

5 Your feathers are as glossy as ebony (line 7)

6 a darted
b sadly

7 a caught / court
b in / inn

8 *The phrase means that the fox thought he had a lot of different clever ways of doing things.*

9 [1] mark for each of these (or similar) points:
- The need for us all to have one good, clear plan when approaching a problem
- The need to apply the right / most appropriate action at the right time

10 a an idiom
b *Whatever you do to someone* [1], *in the future the same thing can happen to you* [1].

11 [1] mark for each of these (or similar) points:
- The stork did not react to the fox's cruel joke; she replied calmly (line 10).
- She quickly thought of a way to teach the fox a lesson (lines 1–12).

12 *Each of these tales is trying to teach the reader something* [1]. *A fable is therefore a type of short story that contains a meaning (a moral), which teaches or warns the reader about something* [1].

13 [1] mark for any three of these (or similar) points:
- To show how the fox reacted in different situations
- To show the range of different skills that the fox had (or believed he had)
- To show different characteristics of the fox's personality
- To show that the fox doesn't always win
- to link the three fables together

14 Child's answer should include any three of these (or similar) points; [1] mark for each.
Extract A tells us that the fox is:
- crafty (line 13)
- old (line 1)
- clever (line 16)
- quick to flatter others for his personal gain (lines 6–10)
- happy to cheat others out of their possessions (lines 4–5)
- convinced that he is more intelligent than anyone else (line 16)

Extract B tells us that the fox is:
- eager to boast about his skills (lines 3–4)
- quick to judge others (line 2)
- indecisive (line 10)

Extract C tells us that the fox:
- takes pleasure in playing cruel jokes on others (lines 3–4)
- does not stop to consider the feelings of others (line 3)
- is greedy (line 13)

15 Child's answer should offer an opinion on the character of each animal, e.g.
The fox was right in thinking that the crow was vain because she eagerly accepted the praise without taking the time to consider the fox's motive [1]. *However, the fox was wrong to think that the cat was stupid because it was able to react more quickly than the fox could in the situation* [1]. *The fox was also wrong in thinking that the stork had no feelings, as she was quick to turn the tables on him and teach him a lesson* [1].

16 a cleverest / most beautifully elegant / scruffiest / prettiest
b brightest / stupidest
c tastiest / longest / most wonderful

Paper 5

1 Laurence, Clara, Charley, Alice
2 *Yes, Clara is happy as her voice is described as being 'gladsome'* [1] (line 8) *and a section of the flower-bed had been reserved just for her* [1] (line 9).
3 C, D
4 *The children had all been very busy outside for the afternoon* [1]; *a summer afternoon seemed to them to be extremely long* [1] (lines 15–16).
5 'and to think that, different as they were, the hearts of both could be gladdened with the same joys.' (lines 19–20)
6 [1] mark each for any four of these points: The chair:
   • was made of oak (line 28)
   • was shiny where it had been regularly polished (line 29)
   • was big and heavy (line 30)
   • had a high back that had different shapes carved into it, such as flowers (lines 30–32)
   • had a lion's head carved on the top of it (line 34)
   • was old (line 27)
   • had an interesting history (lines 45–46)
7 a *cut*
   b *wild*
8 a back / head
   b large / heavy / white
   c it
   d above
9 [1] mark each for any two of these similes:
   • like a butterfly (line 12)
   • like a long lifetime (line 16)
   • as bright as mahogany (line 29)
10 *The statement is false; the chair is very old and Grandfather has had it a long time* [1]. [1] mark for including a piece of appropriate evidence such as:
   • The children had seen Grandfather sitting in this chair ever since they could remember (lines 36–37).
   • One of the children possibly thought that Grandfather and the chair had been born at the same time. (lines 37–38)
11 a–c [1] mark each for any three of these homophone sets:
   I / eye; you / yew / ewe; great / grate; stories / storeys
12 [1] mark each for any three of these (or similar) points:
   • They didn't want to go back outside to play (line 15).
   • The children were already sitting around Grandfather's chair (lines 16–17).
   • Alice wanted to go to sleep (line 22).
   • They were interested to find out more about the strange chair (lines 26–27 and 44).
   • They liked hearing adventure stories (line 51).
13 [1] mark each for these three (or similar) points: The phrase implies that:
   • the stories will include secrets that won't be found in any books
   • the stories will be about famous people from the past
   • not all learning can be done through schoolbooks
14 [1] mark each for any three of these (or similar) points:
   • An adventure story (line 51)
   • A secret that nobody else knows or can read about (lines 47–48)
   • A personal memory (lines 45–46)
   • A story that will teach the children something important (lines 47–48)

Paper 6

1 a Fortunate Isles
   b Hyperboreans
   c Mediterranean
   d South
2 Yes, the gods did come down to earth. [1] mark each for including any two pieces of appropriate evidence, such as:
   • 'the gods often went to visit them' (line 8)
   • 'sent his servants, the Furies, to punish men and women' (lines 20–21)
   • 'his father in a fit of anger threw him out of heaven' (lines 26–27)
   • 'when he reached the island of Lemnos' (lines 27–28)
   • 'flowers sprang up where her feet touched' (lines 34–35)
   • 'in her house upon Mount Olympus' (line 40)
   • 'whom Zeus in the form of an eagle carried away to heaven' (lines 61–62)
   • 'Under the waves he had a shining palace' (lines 65–66)
   • 'the road by which she travelled from heaven to earth was the rainbow' (line 71)
   • 'All these went and came as they pleased, being sometimes in the sky, sometimes on earth' (lines 85–86)
3 Zeus
4 The Fortunate Isles (Islands of the Blessed)
5 [1] mark each for any five of these points:
   • She was very attractive (line 22).
   • She was dignified (line 23).
   • Her eyes were like those of an ox – large and dark (line 23).

- She was conceited (line 24).
- She was argumentative (line 24).
- She was prepared to hurt those who angered her (line 24).

6 *Hephæstus was the blacksmith god and he would have needed intense heat and fire to make his metal goods* [1]. *The fire and heat of a volcano would therefore have made an ideal place for him to work in* [1].

7 *This statement is false* [1] *because the text states that 'she made some people happy, but for others she caused much grief and trouble'* [1] (line 35–36).

8 A, C

9 **a** Hermes (Mercurius)
b Demeter (Ceres)

10 **a** *threw*
b *scraps*

11 brass

12 **a** *The Furies were Zeus's servants* [1] (line 20) *and their job was to follow wicked men and women and whip them as a punishment* [1] (lines 78–79).
b *The Furies looked frightening because of the snakes on their heads* (line 77). *Their role was to scare and punish people, so their appearance fit their job* (line 78).

13 [1] mark each for any eight of these points:
The gods:
- lived mostly above or below the ground (in heaven or the sea) (lines 12 and 65)
- were larger, stronger and more attractive than humans (line 14)
- were able to control nature (e.g. the weather, volcanoes, the sun and the moon, rainbows, harvests, plant growth) (lines 16, 31, 41, 43, 67)
- were born in strange ways (from the foam of the sea or from inside Zeus's head, for example) (lines 33 and 38)
- often had wings and could fly between heaven and earth (line 85)
- sometimes had animalistic features (the Furies had snakes on their head instead of hair, for example) (line 77)
- were able to affect the course of human lives (sometimes helping, hindering or punishing) (lines 88–90)
- ate strange foods such as nectar and ambrosia (line 59)
- could transform into different states (Zeus took the form of an eagle, for example) (line 61)
- could not be killed (line 87)
- had ichor instead of blood in their veins (line 88)

1 'underground passages / regular burrows' (lines 4–5)

2 hunting [1], engineering [1] (line 11)

3 'at the elbow of the tunnel' (line 17)

4 The Tarantula eats Flies [$^1/_2$] and other insects [$^1/_2$] (line 46).

5 **a** barren
b vertical
c watchful
d opening

6 'eyes gleaming like diamonds' [1] (lines 19–20); 'bright as a cat's eyes' [1] (line 20)

7 Arachnid (line 43)

8 The lining material that she weaves onto the walls using her spinnerets (lines 30–31).

9 The statement is false; the spider lives in the desert [1]. This is implied by the following sentence: '… tarantula by preference inhabits open places, dry, arid, uncultivated places, exposed to the sun' [1] (lines 1–3).

10 [1] mark for each point:
- It may have been destroyed by the weather (line 37)
- The spider may not have been able to find the right materials to build it (line 38)
- Only the cleverest and fittest spiders may be skilled enough to build them (lines 39–40).

11 invariably (line 35)

12 [1] mark for each point:
A shaft will act as:
- protection against flooding / bad weather conditions (line 44)
- a barrier to stop foreign bodies and debris obstructing the burrow opening (line 45)
- a platform for her prey to land on (lines 46–47)

13 *The shaft needs to be hollow so that the spider can move easily when striking out at her prey.* [1]

14 'which' or 'when'

15 [1] mark for each of these three (or similar) points:
The spider makes the optimum use of her hunting and engineering skills [1] *to ensure that she has thought about every problem regarding feeding and living in advance* [1]. *Her well-designed home means that she has done as much as she can to secure her survival* [1].

16 *The text suggests that these spiders are very intelligent creatures* [1] *because it states that they:* [1] mark for any four of these (or similar) points:
- are effective hunters (line 11)
- are skilled engineers / architects (line 11), although not true of all Lycosa tarantulas (line 36)

A5

- choose to live out of sight and reach of predators (line 12–13)
- are always alert, watching for prey (lines 17–18)
- are forward-thinking (prepare for any eventuality) (line 14)
- have found a solution to ensuring the stability and cleanliness of their homes (line 33)
- have found a way of living that ensures their survival (line 14)

17 *hard-working, busy, active*
18 *This extract is likely to have been taken from a science resource (a book, website or information leaflet, for example)* [1] *because*: [1] mark for including a piece of appropriate evidence, such as:
- it includes scientific terms such as 'Lycosa tarantula' (line 1), 'diameter' (line 7) and 'perpendicular' (line 9)
- it describes how, where and why a specific spider lives, eats and moves in a particular way
- the narrator sounds like a scientist (he refers to hunting for spiders) (line 19)

Paper 8

1 a–d Egypt, Assyria, Greece, Persia
2 *I would have chosen the arable steppes* [1] *because this area offers lush plains* [1] *that would be ideal for growing and harvesting crops* [1].
3 biting (line 8)
4 6 months (line 9)
5 *Due to the biting wind, the temperature is low enough to turn water into ice for half of the year* [1]. *The water is locked up or imprisoned by the ice* [1]. *The water is only freed in the summertime, when the warmth of the sun brings life back to this area* [1].
6 'the seeding-place of nations' (lines 11–12); 'the home of restless tribes' (line 12)
7 between the Urals and the Caspian Sea (lines 13–14)
8 a a simile
   b 'spreads like a sea' (lines 12–13)
9 a *winding, twisting*
   b *dreams, goals*
   c *angry, irate*
   d *luck, chance*
10 *The mist prevents the onlooker from seeing objects clearly, as it acts like a thick blanket* [1] (line 19). *It gradually thins in parts, uncovering objects at different speeds, which helps to distort shapes* [1] (lines 21–22).

11 [1] mark each for any five of these points:
- The use of eerie imagery such as 'mist' (line 19) and 'shadows' (line 22)
- The use of evocative terms such as 'vague forms' (line 21) and 'monstrous' beings (line 22) of 'unnatural dimensions' (line 24)
- The idea of comparing the land to a graveyard, 'a buried wonderland' (line 22)
- The use of simile, 'like a great white curtain' (line 23)
- The use of metaphors: 'a dense white shroud' (line 19) and 'monsters and giants' (line 26)
- The idea of a magician casting a spell to make the mist disappear, 'an enchanter's wand' (line 25)

12 a East
   b North
   c Scythians
   d West
13 Darius, the King of Persia, invaded their country in 500 B.C.
14 *This extract is likely to have been taken from a historical or geographical resource (a book, website or information leaflet, for example)* [1] *because*: [1] mark for including a piece of appropriate evidence, such as that the extract:
- talks of battles that happened long ago, when few people in the world knew about Russia's existence (line 16)
- uses terms such as 'the mists of prehistoric time' (lines 29–30)
- describes ancient tribes and civilizations (lines 33–34)
- includes a very early date: 500 B.C. (line 42)
- describes the landscapes and position of countries in detail throughout the text

Paper 9

1 1 September 2009 (01/09/09)
2 [1] mark for each point:
- Fallen leaves igniting due to the unusually dry weather and recent heatwave (lines 14–16)
- Someone setting the fire on purpose (arson) (line 18)
- The careless actions of someone camping in the forest (line 18)
3 alliteration
4 'inferno' (line 14); 'blaze' (line 13); 'flames' (line 7)
5 [1] mark each for any three of these points: Fireworks could start a fire that could:
- destroy a whole woodland (lines 40–41)
- spread quickly, burning ancient trees in minutes (lines 42–44)
- kill a wide range of wildlife (lines 46–48)
- leave wildlife homeless (lines 48–49)

6 *It is likely that Extract A has been taken from a newspaper because*: [1] mark for including any five of these points:
The article:
- is set in columns
- has a slogan heading
- includes a date and by-line (reporter details)
- presents an unemotional, factual report of events
- includes external quotes from interviews
- follows a clear paragraph structure
- is written in full sentences and Standard English

7 *He sold fireworks to an under-age child* (lines 8–9).

8 *Other shopkeepers* [1]*, who might also be considering selling fireworks to children illegally* [1].

9 D (lines 5–6)

10 *Sparkless believes that it should be illegal to sell fireworks to any member of the public, not just people who are under 18.*

11 a *carried out*
b *people*

12 [1] mark for any two of these points:
- The fumes from the smoke are described as 'toxic' (line 2)
- The fumes from the smoke are described as 'noxious' (line 6)
- When coming out of the house, Madison appeared confused (line 6)
- Breathing in the smoke had made Madison feel sleepy (lines 24–25)
- Madison had to stay in hospital for observation (lines 26–27)

13 *The wet chair extinguished the flames* (lines 20–21)

14 [1] mark for each point:
- He found a box of matches in a kitchen cupboard.
- There was a lot of discarded paper in the hallway that caught light quickly.

15 Child's answer may agree or disagree with the statement. [1] mark each for any four points that are valid and supported by evidence, such as:
I agree with the statement because:
- he often played in a derelict house, which can be dangerous
- he decided to start a fire inside where there was a lot of paper and furniture that could catch alight
- he took his young sister to the house regularly
- at 13, he was possibly old enough to know better

I disagree with the statement because:
- he did light the fire, but only to keep them all warm – he wasn't trying to burn the house down
- when he saw that the exit was blocked by smoke, he acted quickly to break the window
- he instructed Meera to go and get help
- he realised that something was wrong with Madison and pulled her out of the window
- he spoke clearly and calmly to the police officer, telling her what she needed to know

16 [1] mark each for any five points that are valid and supported by evidence, such as:
- Forest fires can have devastating effects (Extract A)
- Forest fires are a danger to humans, wildlife and woodland (Extract A)
- Don't play with fireworks – it is illegal for children to buy them (Extract B)
- Fireworks can cause serious injuries (Extract B)
- Don't play with matches (Extract C)
- It isn't just the flames of a fire that are dangerous; fumes can be toxic and smoke can block your exit (Extract C)
- Don't attempt to build fires (Extract A and C)
- Fires can spread quicker than you realise (Extract A and C)

Paper 10

1 four

2 D (lines 18–19), E (lines 16–17)

3 a Sir Ban
b Carlion
c gryphons

4 he listened to Merlin's wise words [1] (lines 5–6); he was aided by his sword Excalibur [1] (lines 6–7)

5 *He remembered his disturbing dream when he woke up* [1]*, so he went hunting to try to forget about it* [1].

6 *To prove his hunting skills* [1]*, the King picked the hart as his target to pursue* [1].

7 a he / them
b under / of
c till / and

8 [1] mark for each point:
- It would be a pointless journey for the King, as only Pellinore or a member of his family will be able to capture and kill the beast.
- The King quickly offers to take up the pursuit of a dangerous beast without knowing the full facts.

- The King would be unlikely to catch up with it, if Pellinore has yet to kill it after pursuing it for a year.

9 **a** *considered*
  b *howling*
  c *mission*
  d *image*, *shape*

10 **a** *If a root word ends in a 'y' in the present tense, change the 'y' to 'ied' to form the past tense.*
  b reply (line 39) spy (line 25)

11 twelve months (a year)

12 Uther Pendragon and Lady Igraine

13 *Merlin foresaw Arthur's death as one that would be fitting for a king – to die in battle, possibly fighting his nephew* [1]. *In comparison, he believed his own death would be shameful because he would be buried alive* [1].

14 **a** twelvemonth
  b bade
  c fourscore

15 *Yes, the text implies that this extract is taken from an adventure story* [1]. [1] mark for including any three pieces of appropriate evidence; such as:
The text:
- opens by talking of battles (line 1)
- includes details of a magic sword (line 7)
- describes a fast-paced hunt (lines 25–28)
- includes details of a quest for a strange beast (lines 39–47)
- describes one of the characters as a wizard (line 53)
- implies a great battle is to come in the future, where the King will be killed (line 72)
- sets the action in imaginary places

5 Which phrase suggests that Grandfather was pleased to have Alice sitting on his knee?

B 2

_____

1

6 Describe Grandfather's chair in your own words.

B 3

_____

_____

_____

_____

4

7 Give an alternative for each word as it is used in the text.

B 2
2

   a lopped (line 7) _____   b savage (line 34) _____

8 Find an example of each of the following parts of speech in this sentence.

'It was very large and heavy, and had a back that rose high above Grandfather's white head.'

B 2

   a a **noun** _____   b an **adjective** _____

4

   c a **pronoun** _____   d a **preposition** _____

9 Find TWO examples of **similes** in the text.

B 2

_____

_____

2

10 Grandfather had bought the chair recently. Do you agree with this statement? Support your answer with evidence from the text.

B 2

_____

_____

_____

3

11 Find THREE **homophones** in this sentence. Write them, with their **homophone** partners, below.

B 2

"I can tell you a great many stories of my chair."

   a _____ / _____   b _____ / _____

   c _____ / _____

3

12 Why do you think the children wanted Grandfather to tell them a story?

_____

_____

_____

_____

13 What do you think Grandfather means when he says that the stories would teach Laurence "something about the history and distinguished people of his country which he has never read in any of his schoolbooks" (lines 47–48)?

_____

_____

_____

_____

14 What type of story do you think Grandfather will tell? Use the text to support your answer.

_____

_____

_____

_____

Now go to the Progress Chart to record your score! **Total** 35

The Gods of Greece

The Greeks believed that the world was round and flat. Its outer border was the great river, Ocean. The Mediterranean Sea was in the centre of this circle.

Far to the North lived the Hyperboreans in a beautiful land where cold winds did not blow and snow never fell. These people were not obliged to work, and they had no enemies with whom to fight. Sickness and old age did not trouble them. Their 5
lives were happy and tranquil.

In the distant South were the Æthiopians, who were so good and happy that the gods often went to visit them.

In the far-off West were the Fortunate Isles, or 'Islands of the Blessed', where everything was charming, and where a few people, beloved by the gods, lived 10
forever without pain or sorrow.

The Greeks thought there were many gods, most of whom lived above the clouds on top of Olympus, a mountain in Thessaly. They had bodies like men and women, but they were larger, stronger, and usually handsomer than human beings.

The king of all the gods, and the father of many of them, was called Zeus. The 15
Latin name for this god is Jupiter. He was the ruler of the weather. At his command the clouds gathered, rain or snow fell, gentle winds blew, or storms roared. He darted lightning across the sky and hurled thunderbolts upon the world.

The tallest trees and highest mountain peaks were sacred to him.

He was also the god of justice, and sent his servants, the Furies, to punish men 20
and women who did wrong.

His wife was Hera, who in Latin is called Juno. She was very handsome and stately. Her eyes were large and dark, so that one poet called her 'ox-eyed'. She was proud and quarrelsome and ready to harm those who made her angry.

This couple had several children. One of them, Hephæstus, the Latin Vulcanus, is 25
said by some to have been born lame. Others say that his father in a fit of anger threw him out of heaven. He fell for a long summer day, and when he reached the island of Lemnos he had little life remaining in him, and limped forever after. He was the blacksmith god, who built houses for the other gods and made the sceptre of Zeus, the arrows used by Apollo and Artemis, and other wonderful things. He was good- 30
natured and fond of fun, but not foolish. Volcanoes were called his earthly workshops.

His wife was Aphrodite, the Latin Venus, the loveliest of all the goddesses, who was said to have been born from the foam of the sea. She was the ruler of love and beauty. Wherever she went soft and gentle breezes followed her, and flowers sprang up where her feet touched. She made some people happy, but for others 35
she caused much grief and trouble.

One day Zeus had a terrible headache. Hephæstus, with an axe, split open his father's aching head. The goddess Athene, the Latin Minerva, sprang out, full grown and dressed in armour. She became the goddess of wisdom, and also took care of cities. She never married but lived alone in her house upon Mount Olympus. 40

Phœbus, the Latin Apollo, was the god who ruled the sun. He loved music and poetry.

Artemis, the Latin Diana, was his twin sister. She had charge of the moon and was the friend of the hunters.

Hermes, the Latin Mercurius, whence our Mercury, was handsome and swift, the messenger of the gods. Under his care were merchants, travellers, and public speakers. He wore a low-crowned hat with wings, and wings grew from his ankles. In his hand, he carried a wand around which snakes twined. He was very cunning and full of tricks.

Ares, the Latin Mars, was the god of war, finding pleasure in battle and death.

Hestia, the Latin Vesta, was the sister of Zeus. She was the goddess of the fireside and watched over the homes of men. She never married, but Zeus gave her a seat in the centre of his palace and sent her the sweetest morsels at every feast. On earth she was worshipped as the oldest and best of the gods. In her temple a sacred fire was kept forever burning, watched by un-married women, who were called 'Vestal Virgins'.

These ten gods formed the 'Great Council' of Olympus. They lived in their own houses of brass, built by Hephæstus, but every day they went to the palace of Zeus and feasted on ambrosia and nectar. Hebe, the beautiful daughter of Zeus and Hera, waited upon the table. After her marriage to Heracles her place was taken by Ganymede, a beautiful Trojan boy, whom Zeus in the form of an eagle carried away to heaven. At the feasts Apollo played on his lyre and the Muses sang. The Muses were nine sisters, who lived on Mount Parnassus. They had charge of poetry, history, music, tragedy, comedy, dancing, love-songs, hymns, and astronomy.

The ruler of the sea was Poseidon, whose Latin name was Neptune. Under the waves he had a shining palace, the work of Hephæstus.

Demeter, the Latin Ceres, was goddess of the earth, especially of harvests of grain. Dionysus, or Bacchus, was the god of vineyards and wine, and was particularly adored by the Greeks. Eros, the Latin Cupid, the little god of love, was the son of Venus. Eos was the goddess of the dawn. Iris was the messenger of Hera, and the road by which she travelled from heaven to earth was the rainbow, which vanished when her errand was done.

There were three Fates, who spun the thread of human life and cut it off at their pleasure.

There were three Graces, who favoured everything beautiful and charming in manners and dress.

There were also three Furies, who had snakes for hair and were frightful to look at. It was their duty to follow wicked men and women and punish them with dreadful whips.

Nemesis, like the Furies, pursued those who had done wrong, particularly those who had insulted the gods. Wherever she went trouble and sorrow followed. Momus was the god of laughter, Morpheus of sleep, and Plutus of riches. Plutus was blind and could not see those to whom he gave his gifts. When he approached men he limped slowly along. When he left them he flew away.

All these went and came as they pleased, being sometimes in the sky, sometimes on the earth. They did not always do right, and they often quarrelled and fought among themselves. Although they could not be killed, they could be wounded. Then ichor instead of blood flowed from their veins. They took much interest in human affairs; they had their favourites whom they helped, and their enemies whom they tried to harm.

From *Stories of the Ancient Greeks* by Charles D. Shaw

1 Choose ONE word or short phrase from the list below that best completes each of the following sentences.

North   Mediterranean   East   West   Hyperboreans   Æthiopians

Fortunate Isles   Thessaly   South   Ganymede   Mount Parnassus

a The lands to the extreme left were called the _____ .

b The people who lived at the most northern point were the _____ .

c The Greeks believed that the very middle of the world was the _____ .

d The Æthiopians lived to the far _____ .

2 Did the gods ever come down from the skies? Support your answer with TWO pieces of evidence from the text.

_____

_____

3 What is the Greek name for the god Jupiter? _____

4 In which part of the world did some people enjoy eternal life?

_____

5 Write your own description of Hera's physical appearance and her personality.

_____

_____

_____

_____

_____

6 Explain the sentence, 'Volcanoes were called his earthly workshops ...', as used in the text (line 31).

_____

_____

7 Aphrodite was always kind and compassionate. Do you agree with this statement? Refer to the text in your answer.

_____

_____

_____

8 Tick the TWO statements that are false.

B 2

A Artemis was the twin sister of Diana. ☐

B Hermes was crafty. ☐

C Nemesis made people laugh. ☐

D Zeus was the brother of Hestia. ☐

E Hephæstus was Cupid's father. ☐

2

9 If you held one of the following professions during this time, which god would have been most important to you?

B 2

a a trader _____ **b** a farmer _____

2

10 Give an alternative for each word as it is used in the text.

B 2

a hurled (line 18) _____ **b** morsels (line 53) _____

2

11 What material was Apollo's house made from?

B 2

_____

1

12 Reread lines 20–21 and 77–79 about the Furies.

B 2

a Describe the role of the Furies in your own words.

_____

_____

2

b Why do you think that the Furies looked so frightening?

_____

_____

1

13 This mythological extract illustrates several ways in which the Greek gods were different from humans. Explain at least EIGHT of these differences, referring to the text to support your answer.

B 2

_____

_____

_____

_____

_____

_____

_____

8

Paper 7

Chapter 1 The Black-Bellied Tarantula

Lycosa tarantula by preference inhabits
open places, dry, arid, uncultivated places,
exposed to the sun. She lives generally –
at least when full-grown – in underground
passages, regular burrows, which she digs
for herself. These burrows are cylindrical;
they are often an inch in diameter and run
into the ground to a depth of more than a
foot; but they are not perpendicular. The
inhabitant of this gut proves that she is at
the same time a skilful hunter and an able engineer. It was a question for her not
only of constructing a deep retreat that could hide her from the pursuit of her foes:
she also had to set up her observatory whence to watch for her prey and dart out
upon it. The Tarantula provides for every contingency: the underground passage, in
fact, begins by being vertical, but, at four or five inches from the surface, it bends at
an obtuse angle, forms a horizontal turning and then becomes perpendicular once
more. It is at the elbow of this tunnel that the Tarantula posts herself as a vigilant
sentry and does not for a moment lose sight of the door of her dwelling; it was there
that, at the period when I was hunting her, I used to see those eyes gleaming like
diamonds, bright as a cat's eyes in the dark.

The outer orifice of the Tarantula's burrow is usually surmounted by a shaft
constructed throughout by herself. It is a genuine work of architecture, standing
as much as an inch above the ground and sometimes two inches in diameter, so
that it is wider than the burrow itself. This last circumstance, which seems to have
been calculated by the industrious Spider, lends itself admirably to the necessary
extension of the legs at the moment when the prey is to be seized. The shaft is
composed mainly of bits of dry wood joined by a little clay and so artistically laid,
one above the other, that they form the scaffolding of a straight column, the inside
of which is a hollow cylinder. The solidity of this tubular building, of this outwork,
is ensured above all by the fact that it is lined, upholstered within, with a texture
woven by the Lycosa's spinnerets and continued throughout the interior of the
burrow. It is easy to imagine how useful this cleverly-manufactured lining must be
for preventing landslip or warping, for maintaining cleanliness and for helping her
claws to scale the fortress.

I hinted that this outwork of the burrow was not there invariably; as a matter
of fact, I have often come across Tarantulas' holes without a trace of it, perhaps
because it had been accidentally destroyed by the weather, or because the
Lycosa may not always light upon the proper building-materials, or, lastly, because
architectural talent is possibly declared only in individuals that have reached the
final stage, the period of perfection of their physical and intellectual development.

One thing is certain, that I have had numerous opportunities of seeing these
shafts, these outworks of the Tarantula's abode; they remind me, on a larger scale,

Line numbers in right margin: 5, 10, 15, 20, 25, 30, 35, 40

of the tubes of certain Caddis-worms. The Arachnid had more than one object in view in constructing them: she shelters her retreat from the floods; she protects it from the fall of foreign bodies which, swept by the wind, might end by obstructing it; lastly, she uses it as a snare by offering the Flies and other insects whereon she feeds a projecting point to settle on. Who shall tell us all the wiles employed by this clever and daring huntress?

45

From *The Life of the Spider* by Jean Henri Fabre

1 What type of home does the adult Lycosa tarantula live in?

_____

2 Which TWO skills does the Tarantula possess?

_____

_____

3 Where specifically does the spider lie in wait for her victims?

_____

4 What information are you given about the Tarantula's diet?

_____

5 Underline the word in brackets that is closest in meaning to each word as it is used in the text.

    a arid (line 2)   (unpleasant, putrid, luscious, barren, dangerous)

    b perpendicular (line 9)   (vertical, horizontal, parallel, reflective, obtuse)

    c vigilant (line 17)   (fragile, ravenous, distracted, watchful, bold)

    d orifice (line 21)   (section, opening, vessel, corner, block)

6 Find TWO **similes** that the author uses in the text.

_____

_____

7 Other than the words 'Lycosa tarantula' and 'spider', which other scientific term does the author use to describe the creature?

_____

8 What helps to prevent dirt from building up in the Tarantula's home?

_____

9 You are more likely to find a Lycosa tarantula in a rainforest than in a desert. Do you agree with this statement? Explain your answer with reference to the text.

B 2

_____

_____

_____

2

10 Explain, in your own words, the THREE reasons why not all tarantulas' homes will have an outer burrow.

B 2

_____

_____

_____

_____

3

11 Which word, as used in the text, means the same as 'consistently'?

B 2

1

_____

12 Explain why tarantulas build shafts. Support your answer with THREE pieces of evidence from the text.

B 2

_____

_____

_____

_____

3

13 Why do you think the shaft is hollow rather than solid?

B 2

1

_____

_____

14 Underline a **connective** in the following sentence.

B 2

'This last circumstance, which seems to have been calculated by the industrious spider, lends itself admirably to the necessary extension of the legs at the moment when the prey is to be seized.'

1

15 What is meant by the phrase, 'The Tarantula provides for every contingency ...' (line 14)?

B 2

_____

_____

_____

_____

3

16 Lycosa tarantulas are extremely clever creatures. Discuss this statement with reference to the text.

B 2

_____

_____

_____

_____

_____

_____

_____

_____

5

17 The author refers to the spider as being 'industrious'. What do you think this means?

B 2

_____

1

18 What type of source do you think this extract has been taken from? Explain your answer.

B 1

_____

_____

_____

_____

2

The Ancient Scythians

Far over the eastern half of Europe extends a vast and mighty plain, spreading
thousands of miles to the north and south, to the east and west, in the north a
land of forests, in the south and east a region of treeless levels. Here stretches the
Black Land, whose deep dark soil is fit for endless harvests; here are the arable
steppes, a vast fertile prairie land, and here again the barren steppes, fit only for   5
wandering herds and the tents of nomad shepherds. Across this great plain, in all
directions, flow myriads of meandering streams, many of them swelling into noble
rivers, whose waters find their outlet in great seas. Over it blow the biting winds of
the Arctic zone, chaining its waters in fetters of ice for half the year. On it in summer
shine warm suns, in whose enlivening rays life flows full again.   10

Such is the land with which we have to deal, Russia, the seeding-place of
nations, the home of restless tribes. Here the vast level of Northern Asia spreads
like a sea over half of Europe, following the lowlands between the Urals and the
Caspian Sea. Over these broad plains the fierce horsemen of the East long found
an easy pathway to the rich and doomed cities of the West. Russia was playing its   15
part in the grand drama of the nations in far-off days when such a land was hardly
known to exist.

Have any of my readers ever from a hill-top looked out over a broad, low-lying
meadow-land filled with morning mist, a dense white shroud under which everything
lay hidden, all life and movement lost to view? In such a scene, as the mist thins   20
under the rays of the rising sun, vague forms at first dimly appear, magnified and
monstrous in their outlines, the shadows of a buried wonderland. Then, as the
mist slowly lifts, like a great white curtain, living and moving objects appear below,
still of strange outlines and unnatural dimensions. Finally, as if by the sweep of an
enchanter's wand, the mists vanish, the land lies clear under the solar rays, and we   25
perceive that these seeming monsters and giants are but the familiar forms which
we know so well, those of houses and trees, men and their herds, actively stirring
beneath us, clearly revealed as the things of every day.

It is thus that the land of Russia appears to us when the mists of prehistoric
time first begin to lift. Half-formed figures appear, rising, vanishing, showing   30
large through the vapour; stirring, interwoven, endlessly coming and going; a
phantasmagoria which it is impossible more than half to understand. At that early
date the great Russian plain seems to have been the home of unnumbered tribes
of varied race and origin, made up of men doubtless full of hopes and aspirations
like ourselves, yet whose story we fail to read on the blurred page of history, and   35
concerning whom we must rest content with knowing a few of the names.

Yet progressive civilizations had long existed in the countries to the south, Egypt
and Assyria, Greece and Persia. History was actively being made there, but it had
not penetrated the mist-laden North. The Greeks founded colonies on the northern
shores of the Black Sea, but they troubled themselves little about the seething   40
tribes with whom they came there into contact. The land they called Scythia, and
its people Scythians, but the latter were scarcely known until about 500 B.C., when

Darius, the great Persian king, crossed the Danube and invaded their country. He found life there in abundance, and more war-like activity than he relished, for the fierce nomads drove him and his army in terror from their soil, and only fortune and   45
a bridge of boats saved them from perishing.

It was this event that first gave the people of old Russia a place on the page of history.

From Historical Tales: Russian by Charles Morris

1 Russia was north of which FOUR countries?

a _____   b _____

c _____   d _____

2 If you were a crop farmer at this time, which section of the Black Land would you have chosen for your farmland? Explain your answer with reference to the text.

_____

_____

_____

3 Which ONE word does the author use to describe the Arctic winds?

_____

4 For approximately how many months do these winds last?

_____

5 Explain the following section of text in your own words.

'… chaining its waters in fetters of ice for half the year. On it in summer shine warm suns, in whose enlivening rays life flows full again.'

_____

_____

_____

6 Which TWO phrases tell the reader that Russia is the source of many nationalities?

_____

_____

7 Where are the lowlands?

B 2

1

_____

8 Reread the second paragraph.

B 2

   a Which literary technique is included in this section?

_____

   b Write out the relevant phrase.

2

_____

9 Give an alternative word for each of these words as they are used in the extract.

B 2

   a meandering (line 7) _____   **b** aspirations (line 34) _____

4

   c seething (line 40) _____   **d** fortune (line 45) _____

10 Explain, in your own words, why everyday things appear monstrous and distorted (lines 18–28). Refer to the text in your answer.

B 2

_____

2

_____

11 How does the author make the text in the third paragraph sound supernatural? Include at least FIVE pieces of evidence from the text to support your answer.

B 2

_____

_____

_____

_____

_____

5

_____

12 Choose ONE word from the group below that best completes each of the following sentences.

North   East   South   West   Danube   Greek   Scythians

Darius   Black Sea   Persia   Caspian Sea   Russia

a The horsemen from the _____ were fierce.

b The area to the _____ was misty and impenetrable.

c The Greeks cared little for the people they named _____.

d There were rich cities in the _____ of Russia.

○ 4

13 What event saw the Scythians enter the history books?

_____

○ 1

14 In what type of source would you expect to find this extract? Explain your answer with reference to the text.

_____

_____

_____

○ 2

Now go to the Progress Chart to record your score!   Total ○ 35

34

A

Firefighters Fight Forest Fire

Tuesday 3rd September 2009

by Louisa Johnson

This morning, firefighters from the Cheshire fire service were still trying to control the fire that began sweeping through the ancient forestland on Sunday.

Fire chief David Barnsley remarked that 5 his crew had worked tirelessly over the last three days to put out the flames. He added, "The aim of my team has been twofold: to prevent any further damage to the forest and to stop the fire from spreading to nearby 10 homes. It's still too early to say whether people or animals have been caught up in the blaze. We don't yet know the initial cause of the inferno, but the unusually dry weather and recent heatwave could have caused the 15 fallen leaves to ignite. At this stage, we are also not ruling out the possibility of, for example, arson or a careless camper. The fire sprang up like a coiled spring, engulfing several acres within minutes. As a result, we 20 are doubtful that any casualties caught up in the blaze will have survived, but we are continuing our search."

When asked for his view on this devastating event, local resident Mr Morgan, a member 25 of the Woodland Trust, commented, "I walk my dog in my local forest every day and I regularly see smokers flicking cigarette ash without, it seems, a second thought. I have also seen campers lighting open fires in small 30 clearings, groups of people having barbecues in the summer and teenagers setting off their own fireworks and lighting bonfires on Bonfire Night. All of these people have chosen to ignore the warning notices that the 35 Woodland Trust have posted around the area. It is clear that these offenders don't take the time to consider the fact that every match, cigarette end, fire or barbecue ember or firework has the potential to destroy a whole 40 woodland."

Mr Morgan continued, "Some of the trees in this area were over a hundred years old and they have been destroyed within minutes. The forest was also brimming with wildlife: 45 rabbits, birds, foxes, badgers, hedgehogs and squirrels, which have now either been lost to the flames or have been made homeless through the destruction of their habitat."

Cheshire police have issued another urgent 50 public warning, reminding everyone of the dangers of heatwaves as well as general fire safety tips and have also asked all visitors to the county's many forests and woodlands to be extra vigilant. If members of the public 55 come across any further outbreaks of forest fires or see anyone acting suspiciously, they should report the incident at their local police station, fire service, or Woodland Trust office immediately. 60

B

Fireworks Sold to 10-year-old

Jason Jenkins, vendor of 'Newz' in Primrose Crescent, was fined £300 and ordered to pay £200 costs within 28 days when he appeared before Cheshire magistrates. He was prosecuted after a joint council and Cheshire fire and rescue service operation was conducted in the run-up to last year's Bonfire Night. On 27th October, a 10-year-old child volunteer was able to purchase fireworks from the store. Under-18s are banned from buying fireworks. 10

Councillor Derek Jones commented, "This case is a good example of how seriously we take this issue and acts as a warning for other tempted vendors. We will always prosecute anyone who sells fireworks illegally." 15

Shirley Bryan, spokeswoman for Sparkless, the anti-firework lobby, observed, "This is another great day for the many people who want to see a complete ban on fireworks being available to the public." She added, "Children 20 are hurt every year and many fires are directly caused through the sale of fireworks. We want them to be made illegal for all citizens, not just the under-18s."

C

19th November 2008   PC Amarjit Khan 20785

At 20:14 I was called to 119 Harrogate Avenue by Mrs Leona Brahms who reported smelling toxic fumes coming from the direction of the neighbouring property.

On approach, 117 Harrogate Avenue appeared derelict and in a poor state of repair.

Upon closer investigation I found 13-year-old Callum Crockett attempting to pull his sister, 11-year-old Madison, through a downstairs front window amid plumes of black 5 smoke and noxious fumes. Madison appeared confused so I radioed for an ambulance and then ensured that she was comfortable on the front lawn. At this point, Callum calmly confirmed that no other person was in the derelict property; further stating that 10-year-old Meera Davis had been in the property with them but had made an earlier escape to raise the alarm at home. The arrival of Meera and her mother, Mrs Janine Davis of 72 10 Leeds Road, coincided with that of the ambulance. Mrs Davis provided additional address and contact details for her sister, Ms Jodie Crockett; mother to both Callum and Madison.

All three children, accompanied by myself and Mrs Davis, were transferred to Alder Hey Children's Hospital at 20:35. Ms Crockett arrived at the hospital at 21:10. At 21:40 I was able to question both Callum and Meera further about the incident. They informed 15 me that they often play at the derelict house. On this occasion, Callum found a box of matches in a kitchen cupboard and decided to light a fire to keep them all warm in the downstairs front room. He made a heap from the post that littered the hallway and proceeded to light it. The paper caught quickly and the fire soon spread to the remains of the armchair. The flames died out soon after reaching the chair (Callum recalls the chair 20 being wet) but the chair then appeared to emit thick, black smoke which blocked the path to the front exit.

Callum then smashed the front window with a broken table leg, and instructed Meera to crawl out and go for help. It was at this point that Callum noticed Madison becoming drowsy. He acted quickly in order to pull her through the broken window into the air. 25

Meera and Callum were released from Alder Hey at 21:50. Madison is being kept in for observation. Her condition was described by doctors as stable and not critical.

PC Amarjit Khan   19/11/2008 23:42

These questions are about Extract A.

1 What date did the forest fire start?

_____

2 Describe, in your own words, the THREE possible ways in which David Barnsley thinks the fire could have been triggered.

_____

_____

_____

3 Which literary technique is the title of Extract A an example of?

_____

4 Find two **synonyms** for the word 'fire' in the second paragraph.

_____

5 Why do you think Mr Morgan feels that setting off fireworks in woodland is dangerous?

_____

_____

_____

_____

6 Each extract has been taken from a different source. Where do you think Extract A has been taken from? Support your answer with FIVE pieces of evidence.

_____

_____

_____

_____

_____

These questions are about Extract B.

7 What had Jason Jenkins done wrong?

_____

_____

8 What does the phrase 'other tempted vendors' (lines 13–14) mean?

_____

_____

9 Tick the ONE statement that is true.

A Councillor Derek Jones lives in Primrose Crescent. ☐

B John Jenkins had to pay £500. ☐

C Under-18s are banned from entering shops that sell fireworks. ☐

D The council is working with the fire service. ☐

E Everyone who sells fireworks will be prosecuted. ☐

F A 10-year-old was paid to buy fireworks from 'Newz'. ☐

10 Describe, in your own words, what Sparkless believes in.

_____

_____

11 Give an alternative word or short phrase for each of these words as used in the text.

a conducted (line 6) _____   **b** citizens (line 23) _____

These questions are about Extract C.

12 How do you know that the smoke was dangerous? Refer to the text in your answer.

_____

_____

_____

13 What stopped the fire from spreading?

_____

14 Why do you think it was easy for Callum to start a fire? Explain your answer with reference to the text.

B 2

_____

_____

_____

2

15 Callum obviously had an irresponsible nature. Do you agree with this statement? Support your answer with evidence from the text.

B 2

_____

_____

_____

_____

_____

4

This question is based on all three extracts.

16 'Children should be taught about the dangers of fire from an early age.' If you were teaching fire safety to a Year 5 class, what would be the FIVE key points you would want to teach them and why? You can use any or all of these extracts to help you explain your answer.

B 3

_____

_____

_____

_____

_____

_____

_____

_____

_____

_____

_____

5

_____

Now go to the Progress Chart to record your score! Total 35

Paper 10

The Questing Beast

BUT Arthur had many battles to fight and many Kings to conquer before he was acknowledged lord of them all, and often he would have failed had he not listened to the wisdom of Merlin, and been helped by his sword Excalibur, which in obedience to Merlin's orders he never drew till things were going ill with him. Later it shall be told how the King got the sword Excalibur, which shone so bright in his enemies' eyes that they fell back, dazzled by the brightness. Many Knights came to his standard, and among them Sir Ban, King of Gaul beyond the sea, who was ever his faithful friend. And it was in one of these wars, when King Arthur and King Ban and King Bors went to the rescue of the King of Cameliard, that Arthur saw Guenevere, the King's daughter, whom he afterwards wedded. By and by King Ban and King Bors returned to their own country across the sea, and the King went to Carlion, a town on the river Usk, where a strange dream came to him.

He thought that the land was over-run with gryphons and serpents which burnt and slew his people, and he made war on the monsters, and was sorely wounded, though at last he killed them all. When he awoke the remembrance of his dream was heavy upon him, and to shake it off he summoned his Knights to hunt with him, and they rode fast till they reached a forest. Soon they spied a hart before them, which the King claimed as his game, and he spurred his horse and rode after him. But the hart ran fast and the King could not get near it, and the chase lasted so long that the King himself grew heavy and his horse fell dead under him. Then he sat under a tree and rested, till he heard the baying of hounds, and fancied he counted as many as thirty of them. He raised his head to look, and, coming towards him, saw a beast so strange that its like was not to be found throughout his kingdom. It went straight to the well and drank, making as it did so the noise of many hounds baying, and when it had drunk its fill the beast went its way.

While the King was wondering what sort of a beast this could be, a Knight rode by, who, seeing a man lying under a tree, stopped and said to him: "Knight full of thought and sleepy, tell me if a strange beast has passed this way?"

"Yes, truly," answered Arthur, "and by now it must be two miles distant. What do you want with it?"

"Oh sir, I have followed that beast from far," replied he, "and have ridden my horse to death. If only I could find another I would still go after it." As he spoke a squire came up leading a fresh horse for the King, and when the Knight saw it he prayed that it might be given to him, "for," said he, "I have followed this quest this twelvemonth, and either I shall slay him or he will slay me."

5

10

15

20

25

30

35

40

"Sir Knight," answered the King, "you have done your part; leave now your quest, and let me follow the beast for the same time that you have done."

"Ah, fool!" replied the Knight, whose name was Pellinore, "it would be all in vain, for none may slay that beast but I or my next of kin," and without more words he sprang into the saddle. "You may take my horse by force," said the King, "but I should like to prove first which of us two is the better horseman."

"Well," answered the Knight, "when you want me, come to this spring. Here you will always find me," and, spurring his horse, he galloped away. The King watched him till he was out of sight, then turned to his squire and bade him bring another horse as quickly as he could. While he was waiting for it the wizard Merlin came along in the likeness of a boy, and asked the King why he was so thoughtful.

"I may well be thoughtful," replied the King, "for I have seen the most wonderful sight in all the world."

"That I know well," said Merlin, "for I know all your thoughts. But it is folly to let your mind dwell on it, for thinking will mend nothing. I know, too, that, Uther Pendragon was your father, and your mother was the Lady Igraine."

"How can a boy like you know that?" cried Arthur, growing angry; but Merlin only answered, "I know it better than any man living," and passed, returning soon after in the likeness of an old man of fourscore, and sitting down by the well to rest. "What makes you so sad?" asked he.

"I may well be sad," replied Arthur, "there is plenty to make me so. And besides, there was a boy here who told me things that he had no business to know, and among them the names of my father and mother."

"He told you the truth," said the old man, "and if you would have listened he could have told you still more: how that your sister shall have a child who shall destroy you and all your Knights."

"Who are you?" asked Arthur, wondering.

"I am Merlin, and it was I who came to you in the likeness of a boy. I know all things; how that you shall die a noble death, being slain in battle, while my end will be shameful, for I shall be put alive into the earth."

There was no time to say more, for the man brought up the King's horse and he mounted, and rode fast till he came to Carlion.

From *King Arthur: Tales of the Round Table* edited by Andrew Lang

1 How many kings are mentioned in the extract?

_____

2 Tick the TWO statements that are true.

A The King's enemies were stabbed by his sword. ☐

B Guenevere married King Bors. ☐

C Sir Ban was dazzled by Excalibur's brightness. ☐

D King Bors lived abroad. ☐

E The King of Gaul helped the King of Cameliard. ☐

3 Choose ONE word or short phrase from the group below that best completes each of the following sentences.

> the hart   Arthur   Guenevere   King Bors   Excalibur   Merlin
>
> Sir Ban   Carlion   Usk   gryphons   hounds   The Knight

a The King of Gaul was called _____ .

b The town on the river Usk was called _____ .

c In the dream, the land was over-run with _____ .

4 Give TWO reasons why Arthur was successful in battle.

_____

_____

_____

5 Explain why the King chose to go hunting. Support your answer with evidence from the text.

_____

_____

_____

6 What is meant by '... the King claimed as his game ...' (line 26)?

_____

_____

_____

7 Find an example of each of the following parts of speech in this sentence.

'Then he sat under a tree and rested, till he heard the baying of hounds, and fancied he counted as many as thirty of them.'

a a **pronoun** _____   **b** a **preposition** _____

c a **conjunction** _____

8 Why did Pellinore call the King a fool?

_____

_____

_____

9 Give an alternative for each word as it is used in the text.

    a acknowledged (line 3) _____   **b** baying (line 29) _____

    c quest (line 42) _____   **d** likeness (line 54) _____

B 2
4

10 In the extract, the word 'fancied' is written in the **past tense** (line 29).

    a Which grammar rule must be applied to the **present tense** form of this word to change it into the **past tense** as shown?

_____

_____

B 2
2

    b Find another word in the text that has followed this rule. Write the word in its **present tense** form.

_____

1

11 For how long did the King intend to pursue the beast?

_____

B 2
1

12 Who were Arthur's parents?

_____

B 2
1

13 Explain, in your own words, the difference between how Merlin foresaw Arthur's death and his own.

_____

_____

_____

_____

B 2
2

14 This extract is not taken from a modern text. Find ONE word or short phrase in each of the sections listed below that supports this statement.

    a (line 43) _____   **b** (line 52) _____

    c (line 62) _____

B 2
3

15 This extract is from an adventure story. Do you agree with this statement? Support your answer with THREE pieces of evidence from the text.

_____

_____

_____

_____

B 1
3

Progress Chart   Fourth papers in Comprehension

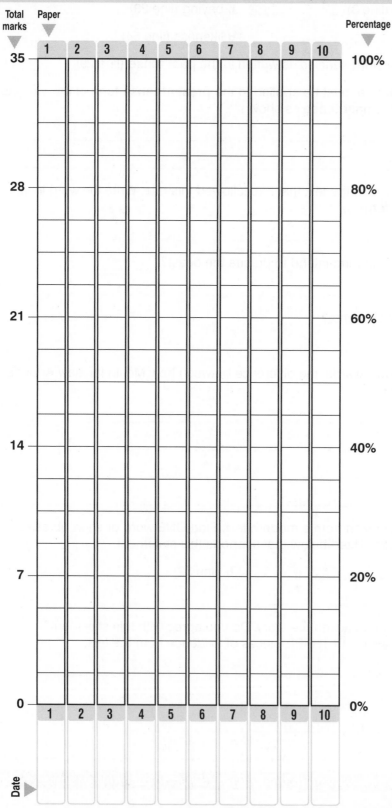

Total marks ▼

Paper ▼

| | 1 | 2 | 3 | 4 | 5 | 6 | 7 | 8 | 9 | 10 |

Percentage ▼

35 — 100%

28 — 80%

21 — 60%

14 — 40%

7 — 20%

0 — 0%

| 1 | 2 | 3 | 4 | 5 | 6 | 7 | 8 | 9 | 10 |

Date ▶

When you've finished the book use the Next Steps Planner ➔